For Mom and Dad who always
encouraged me to achieve my
dreams

Little Mouse and the Dinner

Written and illustrated

by

Raelyn Maxwell

Once upon a time, deep in the thick, green Oak Forest, there lived a little mouse. She was so sweet and caring that all her neighbors in the forest loved her dearly. She was very small, even for a mouse, so everyone called her "Little Mouse."

Little Mouse heard there would be a new addition arriving in their lovely neighborhood.
"I shall prepare a delicious meal to welcome our new friend to the forest," she thought excitedly.

Little Mouse spent the rest of her afternoon writing dinner invitations. She asked her closest friends to bring their favorite foods to a dinner party welcoming their new neighbor.

When the day for the dinner party finally arrived, the weather was perfect. There wasn't a cloud in the sky. Little Mouse was as busy as a bee preparing for her fun event. She was so excited to share a relaxing meal with all her friends that she made a bit too much to eat.

The first to arrive was Little Mouse's friend, Ms. Hen.
"Hello Little Mouse. I'm here for dinner and I've
brought some tasty berry pie," Ms. Hen called
cheerfully while knocking at the door.

"Welcome, my friend. Thank you, what a fun dessert for
us all," Little Mouse exclaimed, opening the door for her
friend to enter. The two sat down at the beautifully set
table and waited for the next guest to arrive.

Soon after, there was another knock at the door. It was Mr. Sparrow.

"Little mouse, it's me, Mr. Sparrow. I'm here for dinner," he tweeted. "I've brought some fresh seeds with me to share with our friends."
"How kind of you. Thank you, Mr. Sparrow," Little Mouse said as she opened the door. Then she set the seeds on the dinner table.

The three chatted for a bit, waiting for the next guest to
arrive.
It wasn't a long wait, and Ms. Squirrel stepped in carrying a
basket full of all sorts of nuts.

"Little Mouse, I'm sorry I'm late. I hope I didn't miss the
chance to welcome our new friend," Ms. Squirrel tittered
anxiously.
"Nonsense. You are right on time," Little Mouse reassured her.
"Oh good! I've brought some seasoned nuts to share
for dinner," she said as she passed the basket to Little Mouse.

The four friends waited around the dinner table. They listened to Little Mouse's wooden clock tick the time away as they watched the minute hand slowly move around the small numbers.

"Goodness, I hope our guest arrives soon. The food is getting cold," Ms. Hen clucked. She looked at the many meals spread around the table and then back at the silent door.

"I'm sure Mr. Fox will arrive shortly. He probably got busy somewhere just as Ms. Squirrel did," Little Mouse said gently.

Gasps echoed all around as each of Little Mouse's friends' eyes widened and their mouths gaped open. Ms. Squirrel began to tremble, and Ms. Hen turned even more pale than her white feathers.

M-Mr. F-Fox?" Mr. Sparrow stuttered nervously. "W-we didn't know w-we would b-be greeting a f-fox."
The others nodded reluctantly in agreement and hastily glanced around the room, as if searching for an exit.
Little Mouse was shocked. "I thought you would like a new friend! Mr. Fox is just like us. He needs a few friends to welcome him into their lives," she said sadly. "I assumed you all would be kind and welcome him as I did for you when we first met."

Just as the three were about to reply, a shadowy figure appeared outside Little Mouse's green curtains. The shadow had pointy ears and razor-sharp teeth. A feeling of dread spread through Little Mouse's home.

The shadow crept around the corner until it could no longer be seen through the curtains. They all listened quietly as footsteps echoed through the wooden cottage.

The footsteps stopped outside the front door. The three friends sucked in their breath. They could only hear the sound of each other's thumping hearts as a muted thud knocked against the door.

The sound carried through the small room. Little Mouse
reached for the door handle, ready to welcome the
visitor.

"No! Don't open it!" Ms. Hen cried in fear, but it was too late.
Little Mouse had opened the door.
Standing in the doorway was a tall orange figure with a paper
bag where his head should be. Ms. Hen stumbled dizzily
backwards at the towering sight.

Just then, a small, round face with a pointed muzzle
popped out around the side of the brown paper bag.
"I'm terribly sorry madam," the orange fox said in a thick
accent.

"My paws are quite full, so I had no other way to knock on
your door other than to hit it with my tail."
The fox peered around the room at all the startled faces.
Then his ears drooped sheepishly as he set the paper bag on
the ground.

"I was not sure what to bring, so I pick out a few things I thought you would like. I hope I didn't scare anybody," he said with a hint of sadness in his voice.

He tried to give the friends a smile, but stopped when they flinched at his toothy grin. "That's alright. I'm probably" too late for dinner now," he sighed. Bending down, he picked up the bag, but was stopped by Ms. Squirrel. "We were just a bit surprised," she said shyly.

Little Mouse smiled with glee, "Please come in, friend. We have been waiting to start dinner."

The fox's eyes lit up with joy as he stepped into the room. Ms. Hen and Mr. Sparrow approached the fox and gave him a sweet but cautious smile. Little Mouse loved seeing her friends warming up to Mr. Fox. She was so glad that they had changed their minds.

The five then sat around the table to enjoy the food. They chatted and laughed and soon they talked as if they had known each other for years. Little Mouse was grateful that they had opened their hearts to a new found friendship.

With all of the food that was prepared, no one went hungry. Even Mr. Fox's larger appetite was filled. That day, each of them left with a full stomach, a bright smile, and a new friend.

The End

Special thanks to my family, friends, and creative writing teacher for their endless support and encouragement during the creation of this book. I couldn't have done it without you!

About the Author

Raelyn Maxwell is a young teen living in St. Augustine, Florida. She is an avid reader, artist, and inspired baker. While working on a creative writing project at school, the idea of *Little Mouse and the Dinner* was born. Raelyn then developed each illustration in her story using an artistic, crayon-like medium. Over a year's time, her school project evolved into the book you are reading now. She never thought it possible one day she could share it with children everywhere. Just like the delicious creations she bakes, this treat is presented to you with a full measure of imagination, just the right amount of thoughtfulness, and more than a pinch of love. She hopes you and your child will enjoy the read and her beloved illustrations. Stay tuned for other books she releases.